IGNITE

30 DAYS TO LAUNCH YOUR FRESHMAN YEAR

START FAST. BUILD MOMENTUM FROM DAY ONE.

JAMES MCLAMB

Ignite: 30 Days to Launch Your Freshman Year

Publisher Information:
James McLamb/Generation Youth
Raleigh, North Carolina

For more information or to contact the author, please visit generation-youth.com or email james@generationziglar.com.

ISBN 979-8-89165-279-8 (softcover)
ISBN 979-8-89165-280-4 (eBook)

Cover design: Abigael Elliott
Interior design: eBookBurner Technologies

First printing: 2025
Printed in the United States of America

TABLE OF CONTENTS

How to Use This Journal v

Before You Begin: Why This Journal Exists ix

Week 1: MINDSET – "Own Your Outlook"..................... 1

Week 2: SELF-IMAGE – "See Yourself Clearly" 35

Pause. Breathe. Laugh A Little. 65

Week 3: RELATIONSHIPS – "Find Your People" 67

Week 4: GOAL SETTING – "Shape Your Future" 97

Final Thoughts from Me to You 139

▨ HOW TO USE THIS JOURNAL

(And Launch Your Freshman Year the Right Way!)

Hey there—welcome! However this journal found its way into your hands—maybe a teacher handed it to you, a parent slid it onto your desk, or maybe you picked it up thinking, *"Might as well start strong"—*I'm really glad you're here.

This journal was created **just for freshmen**. It's not about being perfect. It's about being real, staying grounded, and starting your high school journey with direction. You've got a full year ahead—but these next 30 days? They're the launchpad.

Let's walk through how to use this thing:

▦ USE IT DAILY (OR AS ASSIGNED)

Each day is one entry. That's it. Just one short section a day—enough to spark reflection and build momentum. If your teacher gives you a schedule, follow it. If not, find a moment each day (before school, after class, before bed) that works for you and stick with it. You don't have to do it perfectly—you just have to show up.

READ THE DAILY QUOTE

At the top of each day, you'll find a quote. Some are from legends like Zig Ziglar or Maya Angelou, others might be athletes or everyday folks who've lived through some stuff. These are quick bursts of truth to make you think and fuel your mindset.

 ## REAL LIFE, REAL TALK

Next is a short story. This might come from my own freshman experience (yep—I was once a confused freshman too), someone I taught, or someone I met on this journey. You'll see wins, wipeouts, awkward moments, and everything in between. Why? Because *that's real life.*

 ## TRUTH TO STAND ON

This section breaks down the day's lesson in a straight-to-the-point way. These are mini life lessons about mindset, confidence, self-image, relationships, and goal setting. You don't need to memorize them—just let them shape how you think and move through the year.

 ## YOUR TURN TO REFLECT

Now it's on you. No pressure—just space. Two journal prompts each day give you a chance to think, react, and process. You can write one sentence or a full page. Doodle in

the margins. Be messy. Be honest. This isn't homework—it's your headspace.

⚒ IT'S A TOOL, NOT A TASK

This isn't something to check off a list just to say you did it. This is a tool to help you notice things about yourself, your world, your potential. Some days will hit harder than others. That's normal. Keep going. That's where the growth happens.

🧳 KEEP IT CLOSE

Backpack. Binder. Locker. Nightstand. Wherever you'll remember it. It's yours. Nobody else's—unless you choose to share it. And if you do, pick someone who listens and lifts you up.

🗣 TALK IT OUT (IF ASKED)

Sometimes your teacher, mentor, or classmate might ask what you wrote or felt. If you're up for it—share. Some of the best moments in life come when someone says, *"Same here."*

🏁 DON'T SKIP THE FINISH LINE

Day 30 is a powerful reflection—and trust me, you'll want to hit that page. You might be surprised by how far you've come and what you've discovered about yourself.

So let's go. You've got more in you than you realize.

This journal is just the start—but it's a strong one.

You were made for more than just surviving high school—you were made to thrive.

Let's light this thing up. 💥

P.S. So yeah, this journal was *made* to help kick off your freshman year—but let's be real: freshman year doesn't always start smooth. Maybe your schedule got switched, maybe you're still figuring out where your people are, or maybe the whole high school thing just hit you like a brick wall. It's okay. This journal isn't going anywhere.

You can start fresh anytime—after a rough week, a bad grade, or one of those "I'm over it" moments. Whenever you're ready to reset, refocus, or just clear the noise in your head, pick this back up. It's not about being perfect—it's about not giving up on making this year your best one yet. High school is a journey. You're just getting started. 👊 🔥

⬤ BEFORE YOU BEGIN: WHY THIS JOURNAL EXISTS

Let's start with this:
You don't need another assignment.
You've got enough stuff to read, write, memorize, submit, and stress over already.
So let me be clear—**this isn't homework.**
This is for **you.**

I didn't write this to impress a principal, check a box, or give you something "positive" to do during homeroom.
I wrote this because **I care about your freshman year**—and not just the grades, the rules, or how fast you can figure out your locker combo.

I care about *you.*
And not just surviving high school...
but actually *thriving.*

✸ FRESHMAN YEAR DOESN'T HAVE TO BE A MESS

Listen, I've seen what happens during freshman year.
I've watched students walk in with big energy—and lose it by October.

I've watched students hide who they really are just to fit in. I've seen confidence get crushed, friendships fizzle, dreams get shelved, and joy disappear because no one ever gave them the tools to start strong.

That's why this journal was born.

It's not full of magic answers. It's not trying to "fix" you. It's just packed with **real talk, practical encouragement, and 30 days of mini-lessons** to help you build a mindset and momentum you can actually carry all year long.

You won't find anything earth-shattering in here—but you *will* find truth.
Truth that can help you see yourself differently.
Think more clearly.
Dream a little bigger.
And take that next step with just a little more confidence.

✹ WHAT THIS JOURNAL *IS*

This is a guide, a launchpad, a flashlight, and a mirror.
Each page is short. Real. And (hopefully) even fun.
You'll read a story. Get a spark. Answer a couple questions.
And somewhere in the middle of all that, you might just realize something powerful:

> You're not alone. You're not stuck. And your future is way more in your hands than you think.

This journal will help you:

- ☑ Take control of your mindset

- ☑ Strengthen your self-image

- ☑ Build stronger friendships

- ☑ Set meaningful goals

- ☑ Stay focused when things get tough

- ☑ And realize that this year isn't happening *to* you—it's happening *through* you.

START WITH A BANG

I wrote this journal to help you start freshman year **right**.
Not just with sharpened pencils and a new hoodie.
But with **purpose, perspective, and power.**

You don't need to have it all figured out.
You don't need to be the smartest, loudest, most popular, most athletic person in the building.

You just need to show up.
Write honestly.
And keep going—even when the day's messy.

This journal doesn't ask for perfection.
It asks for movement.

Progress.
One honest answer at a time.
One brave thought at a time.
One small win at a time.

 ## YOU IN?

If you're ready to make this year not just another grade level,
but the beginning of your greatest story yet—
Open to Day 1 and let's go.

Let's build something unforgettable.
Because you're not just a freshman.
You're becoming something fierce.

And you're just getting started.

WEEK 1

MINDSET — *"OWN YOUR OUTLOOK"*

Weekly Quote: *"You become what you think about."*

– Earl Nightingale

 **DAY 1**

WELCOME:
BECOMING STARTS NOW

💬 **TRUTH TO CARRY**

> "Don't wait for the perfect moment. Take the moment and make it perfect."
> – Zoey Sayward

MY FRESH START: TERRIFIED BUT TRYING

I didn't walk into high school ready to take on the world. I walked in scared out of my mind.

Everything was different. Bigger. Louder. Faster. I had come from a small K–8 school where I knew every hallway and every face. But now I was one of over 1,300 students—and my two best friends weren't with me. They had chosen a different high school, and I felt like I was starting completely alone.

I remember clutching my schedule so tight it crumpled. I was terrified I'd get lost, sit in the wrong class, or worse— have no one to sit with at lunch. That fear didn't go away after the first day... or even the first week. I kept my head down, went straight from class to class, and tried to not look like I had no clue what I was doing. Truth is, I didn't.

People talk about "finding your place," but that didn't happen quickly for me. There was no magical "click" moment. It was a slow, awkward, sometimes painful process. I didn't feel like I belonged. I didn't know who I was supposed to be. And honestly? It felt like everyone else had it all figured out except me.

But I kept showing up. I didn't realize it at the time, but that choice—to keep walking into the building, to keep going even though I felt invisible—*that* was the beginning of becoming. Not instantly. Not easily. But eventually.

REAL TALK: THIS YEAR IS YOUR LAUNCHPAD

You don't have to feel brave to be brave. You don't need to have all the answers on day one. High school isn't about chasing the perfect version of yourself—it's about becoming the real one.

That starts now. Not when you're confident. Not when you know where to sit. Right here, right now. Even if you're nervous. Even if you're scared. Especially then.

Because becoming isn't loud and flashy—it's quiet and gritty. It's showing up, even when you'd rather stay hidden. It's asking yourself, *who am I becoming?* and letting that question guide how you live today.

YOUR TURN TO REFLECT

Take a moment to write honestly. There's no "right" answer here—just real ones.

1. What do I want to become this year—not just achieve, but become?
   (What kind of person do I want to be known as? What habits, attitude, or energy do I want to bring?)

   _____

   _____

   _____

   _____

   _____

2. How do I want people to describe me at graduation?
   (What do I hope my friends, family, and teachers say when they look back on who I was this year?)

   _____

   _____

   _____

   _____

   _____

CHOOSE YOUR THOUGHTS

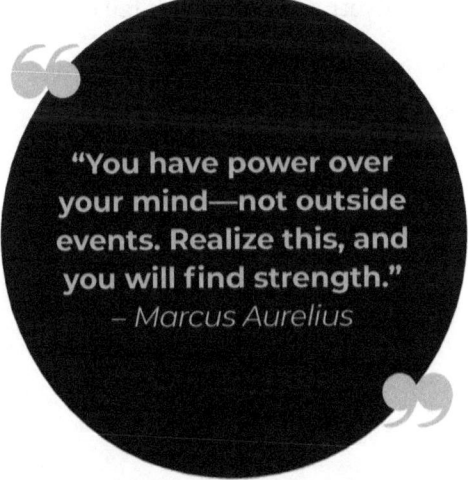

"You have power over your mind—not outside events. Realize this, and you will find strength."
– Marcus Aurelius

MY FRESH START: STUCK IN HER HEAD

When my youngest daughter started high school, her first few weeks were rough—not because of what happened *around* her, but because of what happened *inside* her head.

"I can't get my locker open."
"My friends have different classes."
"Some girls are talking about me."
"The teachers already hate me."
"I'm going to fail."
"I'll embarrass myself."

She was saying it all with a straight face, but I could tell those thoughts weren't just passing through—*they were settling in.* She had convinced herself that high school was already falling apart before it even started.

Here's the wild part: none of it was true.
She figured out her locker. Her friends were still there—just not in every class. The teachers didn't hate her (they barely even knew her yet). And she didn't fail or embarrass herself.

But her *thoughts* had convinced her otherwise.
And those thoughts held her hostage.

REAL TALK: WATCH YOUR INNER NARRATOR

The start of high school hits like a wave—new people, new rules, new expectations. And when it's all unfamiliar, your brain sometimes fills in the blanks with worst-case scenarios. That inner voice? It can either hype you up or hold you back.

Your thoughts are like the narrator of your life story. If that narrator constantly whispers, *"You're not enough. You can't do this,"*—you'll live small. You'll shrink back. You'll miss out.

But here's the good news: *you get to choose the voice you listen to.*

You may not get to pick your classes or schedule—but your thoughts? **Those are yours.**

Start noticing them. Are they helping you breathe easier... or tightening the grip of fear? Are they pushing you forward... or keeping you stuck?

High school is hard enough without your brain being a bully. Talk to yourself like you would a friend—someone worth cheering for.

Because you are.

YOUR TURN TO REFLECT

Take a moment to write honestly. There's no "right" answer here—just *real* ones.

1. What do I want to become this year—not just achieve, but become?

_____

_____

_____

_____

_____

2. How do I want people to describe me at graduation?

_____

_____

_____

_____

_____

✳ DAY 3

GROWTH OVER PERFECTION

💬 **TRUTH TO CARRY**

"Perfection is not attainable, but if we chase perfection we can catch excellence."
– Vince Lombardi

MY FRESH START: DEAR FRESHMAN, WE CAN SEE YOU

As a teacher, I always had to chuckle on the first day of school—especially when the freshmen walked in.

There they were—trying *so hard* not to look nervous. Faking confidence with their extra-straight posture and that look on their face like, *"I totally belong here. I definitely didn't just try to open the wrong locker three times."*

They'd have all their supplies out before the bell even rang. Color-coded folders. Perfectly sharpened pencils. Even a backup pencil—*just in case.* And for the first few days, many of them didn't say much. They were so focused on *not messing up* that they forgot: **nobody expected them to be perfect in the first place.**

The truth is, every teacher who works with freshmen knows exactly what's happening. We know you don't have all the answers. We know you're probably still figuring out what you even need to bring to class, or how long it takes to get from 2nd period to 3rd without speed-walking like you're training for the Olympics.

And that's okay. We expect growth—not perfection. Give me a student who's willing to try, ask questions, and bounce back after making mistakes, and I'll show you someone who's going to crush it by the end of the year.

REAL TALK: MESSY IS PART OF THE PLAN

Here's something no one told me when I was a freshman: *growth is messy on purpose.* You can't "perfect" your way into learning. You *have* to try things that don't work, miss a few steps, and learn to laugh when you trip over your own expectations.

Trying to be perfect all the time is exhausting. And fake. And boring.

Trying to *grow*, though? That's where the good stuff happens.

High school isn't a performance—it's practice. And practice comes with awkward starts, confusing schedules, and days where your locker just won't open (seriously, it's a thing). The question isn't, *"Did I get it right?"* It's, *"Did I learn something?"*

So go ahead and get it wrong. Just don't stay there.
Get back up. Adjust. Ask for help. Grow.
Because progress always beats perfection. Always.

YOUR TURN TO REFLECT

Take a moment to write honestly. There's no "right" answer here—just real ones.

1. When did a failure help me grow?
   (Think about a time you messed up—but learned something important.)

_____

_____

_____

_____

_____

2. What does "progress over perfection" mean to me?
   (How could this mindset help take pressure off and help me grow this year?)

_____

_____

_____

_____

_____

DON'T LET FEAR DRIVE

💬 TRUTH TO CARRY

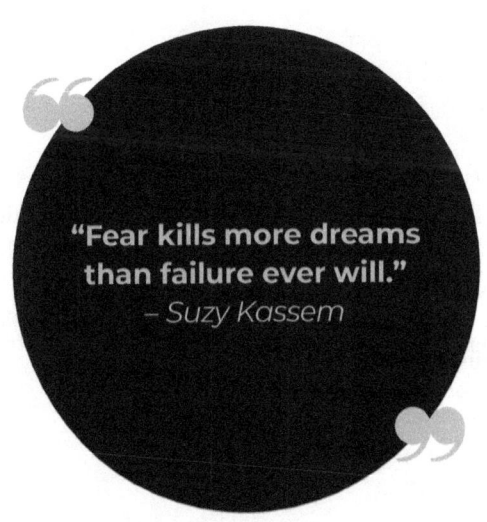

"Fear kills more dreams
than failure ever will."
– *Suzy Kassem*

MY FRESH START: THE CAMPAIGN THAT NEVER WAS

I wanted to be more involved my freshman year. I really did.

I remember seeing the announcement for freshman student government in the first week of school. Something about "representing your class" and "helping plan events." I thought, *Hey, this could be a great way to meet people... maybe even make a difference.*

And then fear came in like a wrecking ball.

My brain instantly launched into full panic-mode:

🎤 *"What if I get zero votes and everyone laughs?"*

🌐 *"What if I mess up my speech, forget my name, and fall off the stage?"*

▦ *"What if they think I'm just a nobody freshman who doesn't belong up there?"*

I pictured shaky posters falling off walls. A microphone squealing. A teacher reading the winners aloud, skipping over my name without even a pause. I convinced myself that trying would just be *one big public failure*.

So, I didn't run. I didn't try. I stayed quiet.
And I regretted it the entire year.

I watched classmates step up and lead. I watched people cheer for them and respect them—and you know what? None of them were perfect. Some stumbled over their words. Some forgot parts of their speeches. One even had their poster misspelled and still got elected.

And all I could think was: *That could've been me.*
If I had just tried.

 # REAL TALK: FEAR ISN'T THE DRIVER

Fear has a way of sounding really convincing. It doesn't yell—it whispers just loud enough to plant doubt. It tells you that trying will end in disaster, that you're not ready, that you're not good enough *yet*.

But here's the truth: **You don't need to be ready—you need to be willing.**
Willing to show up.
Willing to learn.
Willing to fail and still move forward.

Courage isn't about being fearless. It's about being scared and doing it anyway.
That first step might be awkward. It might feel risky.
But what if it's the start of something great?

Don't let fear steal the opportunity you've been wishing for. Try. Speak up. Step forward. You don't need to win to grow—you just need to go for it.

YOUR TURN TO REFLECT

Take a moment to write honestly. There's no "right" answer here—just real ones.

1. What's something I want to try but feel scared to do? (What's been sitting on my heart lately that I keep talking myself out of?)

_____

_____

_____

_____

_____

2. What's one small step I could take anyway? (What would it look like to move forward even if I still feel nervous?)

_____

_____

_____

_____

_____

REWIRE THE INNER VOICE

💬 TRUTH TO CARRY

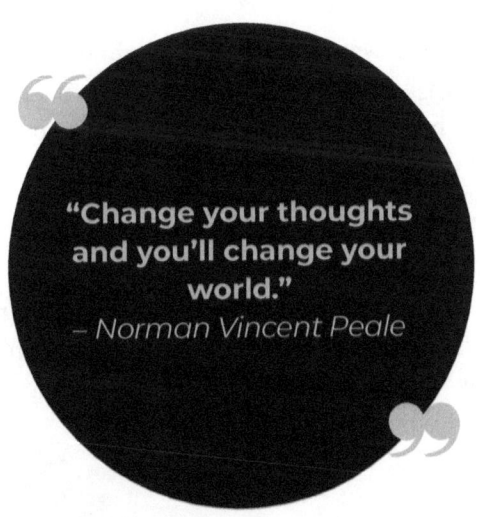

"Change your thoughts and you'll change your world."
– Norman Vincent Peale

MY FRESH START: THE SKINNY KID STRUGGLE

I walked into high school as a 5'4", 115-pound freshman who looked like I had just come off the JV Lego team. Soaking wet, with a backpack bigger than my body, I had absolutely zero idea what made someone "cool"—but I was *very* aware I probably wasn't it.

And then my inner voice started talking. A lot.
Most of it sounded like this:

"You're too small to fit in."
"They're all laughing at you."
"Just keep your head down and survive."

That last one might've been meant as helpful—but honestly, it felt more like hiding than thriving. I was trying to stay invisible while also secretly hoping someone would *notice* me. Talk about emotional gymnastics.

Meanwhile, I watched the tall, confident upperclassmen glide through the halls like they were in a music video. I, on the other hand, was still figuring out how to open my locker without dropping my books... again.

What I didn't realize then was how powerful that inner voice really was.
Every comment it made, every jab or joke, set the tone for how I saw myself. The critic in my head wasn't just being dramatic—it was holding me back. Telling me who I wasn't instead of who I *could become*.

But every once in a while, a quieter voice would break through.

"You'll figure it out—just give it time."

"You're not there yet, but you're learning."

Those moments didn't erase the self-doubt, but they gave me just enough hope to take the next step. And that's all I needed.

 ## REAL TALK: WHO'S DRIVING THE NARRATION?

Your inner voice? It's the narrator of your story. And it's got power.

The words you *say to yourself* shape the way you walk into a room, face a challenge, or talk to someone new.

Some days, your inner voice might be a coach—pushing you to grow, reminding you how far you've come. Other days, it's a critic—nitpicking every little thing, comparing you to everyone else.

Here's the key: you get to **choose which voice to feed.**

If your critic is the loudest voice, it's time to turn up the volume on the coach.

Say things like:

"I'm learning."

"I don't have to be perfect."

"I can do hard things."

Because when your inner voice changes, your pace changes. And when your pace changes... your story starts moving forward.

YOUR TURN TO REFLECT

Take a moment to write honestly. There's no "right" answer here—just real ones.

1. What does my inner voice sound like today?
   (Am I coaching myself forward... or holding myself back with criticism?)

   _____

   _____

   _____

   _____

2. How can I speak to myself with more encouragement?
   (What would I say to a friend going through what I'm feeling?)

   _____

   _____

   _____

   _____

COMPARISON IS A THIEF

💬 **TRUTH TO CARRY**

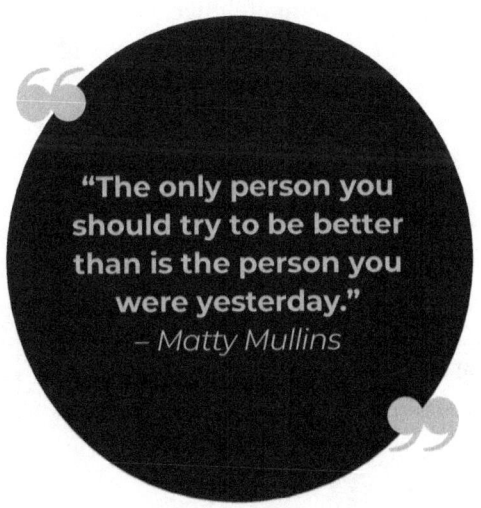

"The only person you should try to be better than is the person you were yesterday."
– *Matty Mullins*

MY FRESH START: THE KIRSTEN & AIME TRAP

Kirsten was in my freshman class, and she was *awesome*. Smart. Kind. Driven. Creative. A total leader in the making.

But she didn't see any of that.
Not because it wasn't true—but because she was too busy looking at Aime.

Aime was also smart. Also kind. Also a leader. And in Kirsten's eyes, Aime had it all—great grades, friends who adored her, and the kind of magnetic personality that made walking into a room look effortless.

Kirsten didn't *hate* Aime. But she envied her. Quietly. Deeply.
And in her mind, it wasn't enough to be *good*—she had to be *better*.

If Aime got an A, Kirsten felt like a failure for her A-minus. If Aime was in the spotlight, Kirsten told herself she was invisible.
If Aime smiled and laughed with others, Kirsten felt like she didn't matter.

Here's the crazy part: Kirsten had *everything* she needed to thrive. But comparison convinced her she was falling behind in a race she didn't even need to run.

And that comparison?
It didn't make her better. It made her bitter.
It stole her joy. It stalled her growth. And it wasn't even real.

REAL TALK: YOU WEREN'T MADE TO BE A COPY

Freshman year is tough—especially when it feels like everyone else already knows who they are. You walk into school and it's easy to zero in on "her"—the girl with the confidence, the crew, the clothes, the sparkle.

You start thinking:
"If I was more like her, I'd be enough."
"If I looked like that, talked like that, lived like that..."

But let's call that what it is: **a trap.**

Your value doesn't increase when you become more like someone else.
You weren't made to be her—you were made to be *you*.
And trying to mimic someone else only hides what makes *your* story so powerful.

Here's the truth: comparison will always steal something—your confidence, your joy, your pace. But identity? That gives. It grounds you. It frees you. It reminds you there's only one person you're supposed to grow into—**you.**

YOUR TURN TO REFLECT

Take a moment to write honestly. There's no "right" answer here—just real ones.

1. Where do I catch myself comparing?
   (Who or what do I keep measuring myself against?)

   _____

   _____

   _____

   _____

   _____

2. What's something that makes *my* story unique?
   (What strengths, experiences, or qualities are *mine*—no copy, no comparison?)

   _____

   _____

   _____

   _____

   _____

 **DAY 7**

SHOW UP FOR YOURSELF

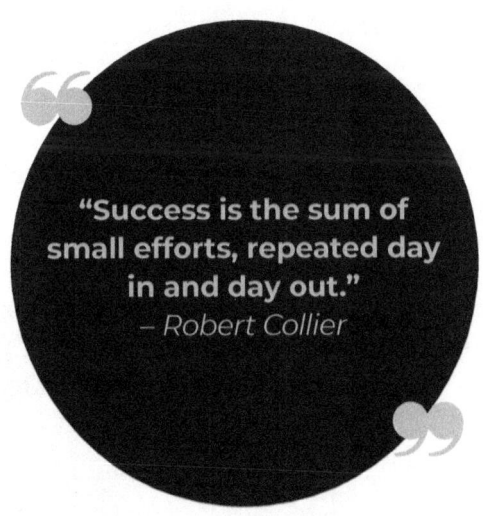

"Success is the sum of small efforts, repeated day in and day out."
– Robert Collier

MY FRESH START: TRYOUT HEROES & TUESDAY SLUMPS

I coached high school baseball for years, and let me tell you—freshman tryouts were something else.

You'd see these wide-eyed 14-year-olds giving *everything* they had. Hustling like their cleats were on fire. Diving for balls like they were auditioning for a sports movie. One kid even slid into first base during *warmups*. It was like watching a Rocky montage—minus the theme music and with slightly more sunflower seeds.

The energy at tryouts? ⬤ Unmatched.
But fast forward a few weeks into the season... and some of those same guys were suddenly jogging instead of sprinting. Missing grounders they could've fielded in their sleep. Talking more about what snacks were in the dugout than how to improve their swing.

What happened? The goal was met.
They made the team—and somewhere along the way, *the hunger faded.*

They didn't stop showing up physically. But mentally? They had already packed it in.
No more pushing. No more adjusting. Just coasting.

Here's the thing: **making the team was the moment.**
Getting better? That's the mission.
And the mission takes daily, gritty, not-always-glamorous *effort.*

REAL TALK: THE HYPE FADES—THE HABITS STAY

Freshman year starts a lot like tryouts.
You come in strong—new clothes, fresh backpack, walking into school like you own the place (or at least know where the cafeteria is). But then... October hits. The sparkle fades. The late nights start stacking. The "do I really need to study for this quiz?" thoughts start creeping in.

This is where the *real* game begins.
Success isn't about being hyped every single day. No one wakes up like,
"Yes! I can't wait to do math homework and eat questionable cafeteria pizza!"

Confidence doesn't show up fully formed—it grows from small efforts, stacked over time.
You don't get strong by lifting a heavy thing once. You grow by showing up again and again—especially on the days you don't feel like it.

So even if your backpack's falling apart, your locker won't open, and your brain feels like it's buffering—**show up anyway.**
Do the work. Ask the question. Keep swinging.
Because *consistency* is where the magic happens.

YOUR TURN TO REFLECT

Take a moment to write honestly. There's no "right" answer here—just real ones.

1. What does it look like for me to "show up" today?
   (How can I give my best, even if I'm not feeling 100% motivated?)

   _____

   _____

   _____

   _____

2. When was the last time I did something hard and didn't quit?
   (What helped me push through—and how can I build on that today?)

   _____

   _____

   _____

   _____

MINDSET REFLECTION: MIND OVER NOISE

💬 **TRUTH TO CARRY**

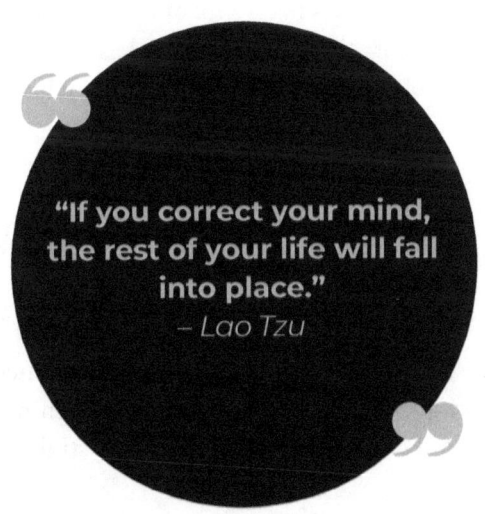

"If you correct your mind, the rest of your life will fall into place."
– Lao Tzu

MY FRESH START: WHO'S RUNNING THE CONTROLS?

Let's be honest—by the end of the first week of freshman year, your brain probably feels like it just ran a mental marathon with no water breaks.

You've tried to figure out where your classes are, how to avoid being the last one in the lunch line, and whether raising your hand in English makes you look smart or try-hard. You've spent the week balancing thoughts like:

🧠 *"Don't trip in the hallway."*

🧠 *"Say something cool."*

🧠 *"Act like you know what you're doing."*

🧠 *"What's her name again?"*

Let's just say—there's been a *lot* of mental noise.
And through it all, your mindset has been working the control panel, deciding what to turn up, what to tune out, and what direction you're headed next.

REAL TALK: MINDSET IS A DAILY DECISION

Some people think mindset is like a t-shirt—once you put it on, you're good to go. But it's more like brushing your teeth: you've got to do it *daily*, or things start to stink.

The truth is, this week was about way more than surviving high school. It was about deciding how you think *about* high school—and more importantly, how you think about *yourself*.

You've had moments where fear showed up. Doubt knocked. Comparison tried to sneak in through the back door.
But you've also had moments of reflection. Growth. Grit.
You've started training your mind to notice when the noise gets loud and to respond with something stronger.

And here's the deal: it doesn't end here.

Next week, you'll still get overwhelmed. There will still be challenges.
But now you've got tools. You've got proof that you can walk through uncertainty, awkwardness, and setbacks—and keep your head in the game.

This week you didn't just learn how to *show up*—you learned how to *show up with purpose*. And that's the kind of mindset that shifts everything.

YOUR TURN TO REFLECT

Take a moment to write honestly. There's no "right" answer here—just real ones.

1. What thought do I want to carry into next week?
   (What belief or reminder will help me keep growing, even when things get hard?)

   _____

   _____

   _____

   _____

   _____

2. How has my mindset shifted already?
   (What's something I see differently now than I did eight days ago?)

   _____

   _____

   _____

   _____

   _____

WEEK 2

SELF-IMAGE — *"SEE YOURSELF CLEARLY"*

Weekly Quote: *"If you really want to fly, harness your power to your passion."*

– Oprah Winfrey

IDENTITY IS NOT A LABEL

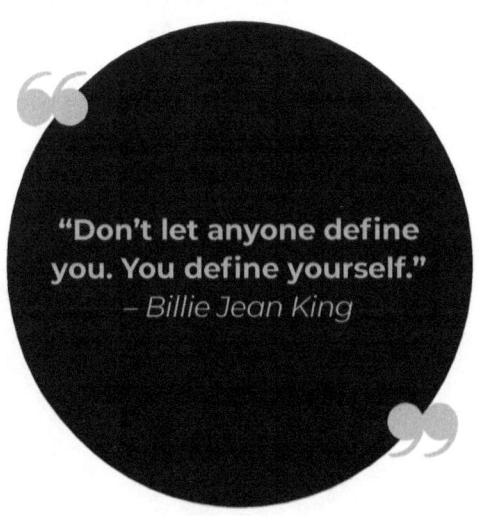

"Don't let anyone define you. You define yourself."
– Billie Jean King

MY FRESH START: STUCK WITH STICKY NOTES

Freshmen get labeled faster than leftovers in a teacher's lounge fridge. And as a teacher? I saw it every year.

A kid would walk into my class and boom—someone in the back row would quietly whisper, *"That's the weird kid from lunch,"* like they were assigning characters in a movie. Meanwhile, a kid who cracked one joke too many on day one? *"Troublemaker."* Just like that. And it stuck.

One year, I had a student named Ryan. Awesome kid. Smart, helpful, funny—but had a bad case of the fidgets. First week, he knocked over his water bottle, tripped over his own backpack, and accidentally erased half the board trying to clean the whiteboard tray.
By week two? "Klutz."
Didn't matter that he later led a group project like a boss and crushed every test. The label stuck—at least in other people's minds.

Here's what I told Ryan, and what I'm telling you:
You don't have to wear what they stick on you.
Not from your classmates.
Not from upperclassmen.
Not even from your teachers.
(Yes, I said it. Teachers are human too. We mess up.)

REAL TALK: LABELS ARE NOT YOUR SIZE

People love labeling freshmen because it's easy. It gives them a shortcut for who they *think* you are: "quiet," "jock," "basic," "geek," "extra," "teacher's pet," "airhead," "try-hard," "slacker," "weirdo."
Heard any of those yet? Thought so.

But let's be real: those labels are lazy. They're someone else's quick guess based on one moment, one trait, or one awkward lunch period. That's like watching 30 seconds of a movie and pretending you know the plot.

Your identity isn't a post-it someone else slapped on your forehead—it's a story you get to write. And guess what? You're still in the intro.

You can be smart and still goof off sometimes.
You can be quiet and still lead.
You can trip in the hallway and still be confident.
(Seriously—hallway tripping is practically a rite of passage.)

So shake off the label. Rip off the sticky note.
And decide: *What do I want to be known for?*
Then start living like *that*.

YOUR TURN TO REFLECT

Take a moment to write honestly. There's no "right" answer here—just real ones.

1. What labels am I done believing?
    (Which words or assumptions from others don't get to define me anymore?)

    _____

    _____

    _____

    _____

    _____

2. What do I want to be known for?
    (If someone described the real me at the end of the year—what would I hope they say?)

    _____

    _____

    _____

    _____

    _____

CONFIDENCE COMES THROUGH ACTION

💬 **TRUTH TO CARRY**

"You gain strength, courage and confidence by every experience in which you really stop to look fear in the face."
– *Eleanor Roosevelt*

MY FRESH START: THE KING OF CRASH-AND-BURN

My freshman year? One word: *chaotic.*
I was like a one-man pep rally for trying new things—and totally bombing most of them.

Trombone solo auditions? Let's just say, my playing sounded more like a goose in distress than a jazz solo.
Sports tryouts? I showed up sweaty, nervous, and hustling like it was the Olympics. Gave it everything... and got cut.
Speaking contests? Signed up. Got on stage. Brain froze. Words tripped. Judges blinked in slow motion. Painful.
Class competitions? Jumped in headfirst. Crashed out by round one.
Asking girls to dances? Oh man—each invite was an act of sweaty, heart-pounding bravery... followed by a very polite "no" or the classic *"uhhh, maybe?"* (which always meant no).

Each miss felt like a neon sign flashing *"NOT GOOD ENOUGH."*
And I started to wonder: **Shouldn't confidence come before you try something?**

Spoiler alert: **it doesn't.**
Confidence doesn't show up first—it *shows up later,* after you've face-planted and still stood back up.

REAL TALK: ACTION BUILDS CONFIDENCE, NOT PERFECTION

Freshman year is weird. You're figuring out who you are while everyone else seems like they've already got their act together (even though *they don't*). It's easy to think, *"Once I feel more confident, I'll try out. Speak up. Say something."*

But that's backward.

Confidence isn't something you wait for—it's something you *build*.
One awkward audition.

One missed shot.
One shaky moment of *"I'm doing it anyway."*

Each step you take, even when it ends in disaster, is stacking something stronger inside you.

You're not going to feel brave every time. And you definitely won't always nail it.
But if you keep showing up, keep risking a little embarrassment, keep trying when it's easier to sit out— you *will* grow. And people will notice—not because you're perfect, but because you're *real*.

You don't need a flawless track record to be confident.
You just need to keep stepping in—even if you're still shaking.

YOUR TURN TO REFLECT

Take a moment to write honestly. There's no "right" answer here—just real ones.

1. When did I step out of my comfort zone?
   (What's something I did even though I was nervous or unsure?)

   _____

   _____

   _____

   _____

   _____

2. What's one way I can stretch myself today?
   (What action could I take that would build real, lasting confidence?)

   _____

   _____

   _____

   _____

   _____

OWN YOUR VOICE

💬 **TRUTH TO CARRY**

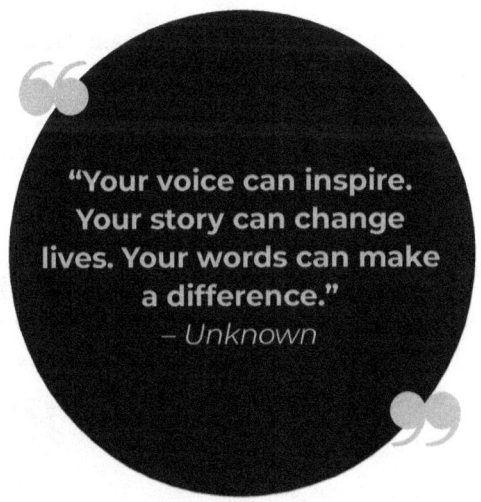

"Your voice can inspire. Your story can change lives. Your words can make a difference."
– *Unknown*

MY FRESH START: CLARK, THE QUIET DIFFERENCE

Clark was one of those freshmen you almost missed if you weren't paying attention.

Quiet. Thoughtful. Kind of wiry. Definitely not the kid making noise in the hallway or trying to impress the crowd. But what stood out—if you really watched—was that Clark *tried*.

He made the soccer team and gave it everything he had. But after a couple of rough games, you could see his confidence slipping. Missed goals? He'd mutter about quitting.

He entered a poetry slam—wrote something raw and honest—but after stumbling through his first reading, he stayed silent the rest of the event.

A science fair project fizzled out—literally—and he played it off like it didn't matter, even though you could tell it did.

Clark was caught in the tension so many freshmen feel: *"If I'm not winning, maybe I shouldn't be speaking."*
But that wasn't true. Not for him. Not for anyone.
And I told him that. I told him, *"You don't need a trophy to have a voice."*

What happened next was small—but powerful.

After a tough soccer game, Clark spoke up during a team debrief. He didn't give a speech—he just vented about how hard he'd worked and how frustrating the game felt. It wasn't polished. But it was *real*.

And the guys listened. They nodded. A few even jumped in with their own thoughts.

Another time, he read a poem—quiet, honest, about feeling invisible. It wasn't a performance. It was a moment of truth. A classmate in the back, one who rarely said anything, raised a hand and said, *"That hit home."*

Clark didn't suddenly become loud or famous or "cool." But something shifted:
He started **owning his voice.**
Not because he won.
But because he stopped waiting for permission.

REAL TALK: YOU DON'T NEED PERMISSION TO MATTER

Here's what Clark—and so many freshmen—need to hear:
Your voice matters before you feel ready.
It matters even when you mess up.
It matters even if you're still figuring things out.

Too many people wait for confidence to show up *before* they speak up. But confidence *comes* from showing up.
From saying something real, even if your voice shakes.
From speaking not to impress, but to connect.
That's when people really listen.

You don't need a perfect moment or a big win.
You just need to be willing to use your voice.
Because someone else might be waiting to hear exactly what *you* have to say.

YOUR TURN TO REFLECT

Take a moment to write honestly. There's no "right" answer here—just real ones.

1. Where have I stayed silent when I wanted to speak up? (What moment passed me by because I doubted my voice?)

   _____

   _____

   _____

   _____

   _____

2. What's something I care deeply about? (What matters to me enough that I'd speak, even if it's scary?)

   _____

   _____

   _____

   _____

   _____

BE KIND TO THE MIRROR

"Beauty begins the moment you decide to be yourself."
– Coco Chanel

MY FRESH START: HAIRSPRAY AND HALFTIMES

My wife has been a cheer coach for both middle school and high school—and let me tell you, she sees *everything*. Not just the stunts and halftime routines. She sees what's really going on with freshmen, especially the girls.

She's watched them shuffle into school that first month, eyes glued to the older girls like they've just seen celebrities walk down the hallway. Perfect hair. Confident walk. Flawless outfits like they stepped straight out of a fashion ad. Meanwhile, the freshmen are sweating through their brand-new jeans, trying to smile like they're not panicking inside.

One girl, Lily, used to spend most of lunch in the bathroom mirror. Not eating. Not laughing. Just applying, reapplying, and fixing makeup that didn't need fixing. She thought she wasn't "pretty enough" because some random sophomore guy didn't say hi. Another girl, Emma, laughed along when a senior made a rude comment, then told her friends later that she felt invisible. She didn't feel like she could speak up—like calling it out would just make things worse.

It's not just a "girl thing," either.

Freshman guys do this too. They flex in mirrors (yes, really), use half a can of body spray trying to smell like confidence, and pretend they don't care when deep down, they're sizing themselves up against the upperclassmen who already have a car and a chin beard.

But here's the truth: real confidence isn't in the mirror—it's in the mindset.

And real beauty? It doesn't show up when someone else notices you. It shows up when *you* notice yourself—your weirdness, your passions, your voice—and decide it's worth owning.

 ## REAL TALK: STOP TWEAKING, START BELIEVING

There's nothing wrong with liking your outfit or fixing your hair. But if you're twisting yourself into someone else's shape just to feel "enough"? That's exhausting—and unnecessary.

The most attractive thing in any room? **Confidence and kindness.**
Confidence says, *"This is who I am."*
Kindness says, *"And I don't have to tear anyone down to be it."*

You don't need permission to be seen. You don't need a filter to be valid.
The mirror isn't a judge. It's just glass. And what matters most isn't what's reflected back—but what you believe about the person looking in.

So today, instead of adjusting your image, adjust your mindset.
Look at yourself the way a real friend would. Then go live like that person deserves to be known, heard, and respected.

Because they do.

YOUR TURN TO REFLECT

Take a moment to write honestly. There's no "right" answer here—just real ones.

1. What's something I love about who I am inside?
   (What quality or strength makes me proud—even if no one else sees it yet?)

   _____

   _____

   _____

   _____

   _____

2. How can I show myself kindness today?
   (What small action or thought can remind me that I'm enough, just as I am?)

   _____

   _____

   _____

   _____

   _____

EVERYONE'S INSECURE

💬 **TRUTH TO CARRY**

"To be yourself in a world that is constantly trying to make you something else is the greatest accomplishment."
– *Ralph Waldo Emerson*

MY FRESH START: FAKING IT, FUMBLING IT

I fully subscribed to the *"fake it till you make it"* strategy as a freshman. I didn't have a clue what I was doing, so I just… acted like I did. Chest out, voice louder, jokes flowing like I was the next stand-up comedian.

It didn't really *work,* but it felt like the best option at the time. Turns out, I wasn't alone.

There was this kid, Ryan—a fellow freshman walking into high school with a buzz of nerves and a hoodie two sizes too big. He wasn't cocky. Just hopeful. Unsure. He figured the secret to confidence was pretending he had it already.

So on Day One, he launched Operation Confidence. He strutted up to a group of sophomores, dropped a line he heard in a movie, and waited for the high-fives. Instead, they looked at him like he was an alien. Brutal.
Later, in gym, he loudly announced he could dunk. Spoiler alert: he could not. What followed was a jump, a flail, and a very public lesson in gravity.

The worst part? Not the failed joke or the missed dunk. It was the moment after—when the mask cracked and the real Ryan was left wondering if maybe he wasn't enough after all.

That's the danger of faking it.
It promises confidence but delivers shame when it falls apart.

REAL TALK: EVEN THE "COOL" KIDS GET NERVOUS

Here's what Ryan—and I—needed to hear: **no one feels 100% confident all the time.**

Not the seniors who walk like they own the hallway. Not the upperclassmen with perfect hair. Not even the kid with the smooth one-liners and fresh Jordans. *Everyone's figuring it out.*

The goal isn't to fake confidence. It's to build it—brick by brick—with real, honest moments.

You don't have to puff up or shrink down. You don't have to play a part to belong.

You just have to *show up* as yourself, even if your voice shakes or your joke bombs.

You're not the only one feeling unsure.

You're just one of the brave ones being real about it.

YOUR TURN TO REFLECT

Take a moment to write honestly. There's no "right" answer here—just real ones.

1. What helps me feel grounded when I'm unsure?
    (What calms the nerves and helps me stay true to myself?)

    _____

    _____

    _____

    _____

    _____

2. Who reminds me of my value?
    (Is there someone in my life who helps me feel seen, no matter what?)

    _____

    _____

    _____

    _____

    _____

YOU'RE BECOMING

💬 **TRUTH TO CARRY**

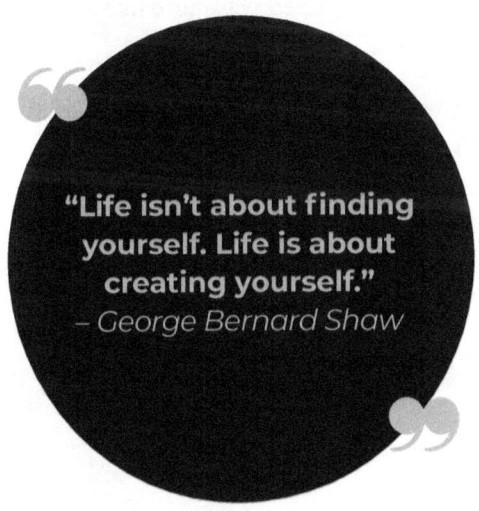

"Life isn't about finding yourself. Life is about creating yourself."
– *George Bernard Shaw*

MY FRESH START: I DIDN'T "FIND" ME—I BUILT ME

If you had met me at the end of my freshman year, you might've said, "Wow, this kid's figuring it out."

But if you'd seen me at the *start* of freshman year?
Total chaos.
I was a walking identity crisis in sneakers too big and confidence too small. I was still recovering from speech contest flops, PE class disasters, and locker combos that felt like secret codes designed to break me.

And back then, I kept thinking, *"Eventually, I'll find myself."* Like one day I'd trip over a metaphorical treasure chest labeled "CONFIDENT, COOL VERSION OF YOU," open it, and just *become* that person instantly.

Spoiler alert: that treasure chest never showed up.

What actually happened was more like a construction zone. I built myself a little at a time.

One awkward moment at lunch where I finally said "hi" to someone new.
One class where I raised my hand even though I wasn't 100% sure I had the answer.
One day where I walked into school not trying to be anyone but *me*.

I didn't "find" myself.
I *built* myself—through every failure, every friendship, every day I kept showing up.

REAL TALK: YOU'RE ALREADY IN MOTION

Here's what I wish every freshman knew: **you're not waiting to become someone—you already are.**
Every class you walk into, every risk you take, every time you bounce back instead of giving up?
That's part of the construction project called *You.*

Freshman year is the start of something, not the final version. You're not behind. You're not broken. You're not missing some magical piece that everyone else secretly has.

You're becoming—**and that's enough.**

So stop measuring yourself against who you think you "should" be. Instead, look at how far you've already come. You've made it through two full weeks of this journal. You've shown up, reflected, written, and probably learned a thing or two about how strong you actually are.

And if you haven't heard this yet: *I'm proud of you.*
Because the you who started this journey? They're already evolving.

YOUR TURN TO REFLECT

Take a moment to write honestly. There's no "right" answer here—just real ones.

1. What am I becoming better at?
    (What's something I've started to improve—even just a little?)

    _____

    _____

    _____

    _____

2. What's one change I've noticed in myself already?
    (Have I noticed more courage, more kindness, more self-respect—big or small?)

    _____

    _____

    _____

    _____

    _____

SELF-IMAGE REFLECTION: WHO YOU ARE BECOMING

💬 **TRUTH TO CARRY**

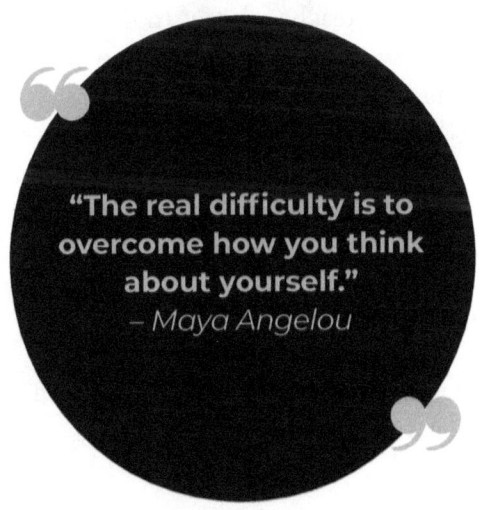

"The real difficulty is to overcome how you think about yourself."
– Maya Angelou

MY FRESH START: LOOKING BACK, SEEING MORE

If you had asked me during my freshman year who I was becoming, I probably would've shrugged and said something like, *"I don't know… hopefully someone who doesn't trip over his own feet in gym class."*

Back then, my self-image was wrapped up in what I *wasn't*. Not tall enough. Not confident enough. Not "cool" enough. I was trying everything—sports, speaking, even school dances—and feeling like I was striking out every time. I thought success would fix my confidence. I thought being "the best" at something would make me believe in myself.

But it wasn't the wins that changed me.
It was the truth I started to believe about myself—even on the days I lost.
That I was brave. That I was kind. That I was becoming.

Years later, as a teacher, I saw those same battles in my students. I saw the freshman girl who wouldn't raise her hand because someone told her she "wasn't smart." I saw the boy who slouched in the back because he thought being goofy was all he had to offer. I saw incredible students—funny, brilliant, creative, determined—*hiding from their own potential* because they believed a lie about who they were.

And now, as someone who speaks to youth across the country, I still see it.
Students searching for their identity in labels, likes, or locker-room rankings.

Trying to be what they think the world wants instead of leaning into who they were created to be.

But the truth?

Your self-image doesn't come from talent. It comes from truth.
It grows every time you choose courage over comfort.
It deepens every time you remind yourself that you are not your mistakes.
It strengthens when you speak life to yourself—not just when things are going great, but when everything feels hard.

You don't need to have it all figured out right now. But you *do* need to decide:
What kind of person do I want to become—and what truth will I build that on?
That's how identity is shaped. One belief. One decision. One day at a time.

YOUR TURN TO REFLECT

Take a moment to write honestly. There's no "right" answer here—just real ones.

1. What positive beliefs about myself are growing stronger? (What am I starting to believe about who I really am?)

   _____

   _____

   _____

   _____

   _____

2. How do I want to continue building my identity? (What kind of character, attitude, or truth do I want to grow more of in my life?)

   _____

   _____

   _____

   _____

   _____

⏸ PAUSE. BREATHE. LAUGH A LITTLE.

Okay. Let's be real for a second.

If your brain feels like mashed potatoes from writing about your thoughts for two weeks straight, congratulations—you're doing it right.

You've made it through 15 days of thinking deep, writing honestly, and showing up for yourself. That's a big deal. Most people tap out before Day 3. You? You're still here. And that *means something*.

But maybe, just maybe, you're starting to wonder:
"Does this even matter?"
"Why does this journal ask so many questions?"
"Can I just nap and hope to become a better person by osmosis?"

Trust me, I get it.
Freshman year is wild enough. This journal? It's like adding emotional squats to your routine.
But that muscle you're building? It's real. And it's strong.

So before we hit Week 3, here's your official invitation to smile at how far you've come—and laugh at how weird this process can be.

Because growth is awkward.
It's tripping over your own shoelaces and realizing—*hey, I'm still moving forward.*

So drink some water. Stretch. Eat a snack that's 73% sugar if needed.
Then get ready to dive into relationships—because things are about to get *real.*

Let's go. You've got this. And I'm proud of you for sticking with it.
We're just getting started.

WEEK 3

RELATIONSHIPS — *"FIND YOUR PEOPLE"*

Weekly Quote: *"Surround yourself with only people who are going to lift you higher."*

– Oprah Winfrey

✳ DAY 16

YOU DON'T HAVE TO DO THIS ALONE

💬 **TRUTH TO CARRY**

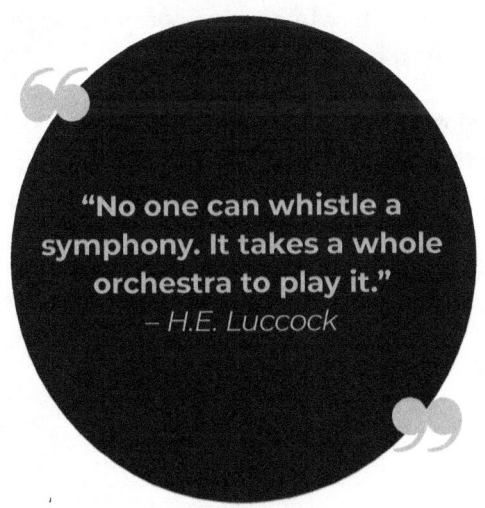

"No one can whistle a symphony. It takes a whole orchestra to play it."
– H.E. Luccock

MY FRESH START: WHERE ARE MY PEOPLE?

Freshman year started with a pretty empty bench.

My two best friends—the guys I'd grown up with for *nine years*—went to a different high school. I had a few familiar faces around, sure, but not the kind of friends you call when life's falling apart or when you need someone to tell you if your breath smells weird before you talk to your crush.

At first, I told myself I'd be fine. I figured if I focused hard enough on school, sports, and pretending I wasn't eating lunch alone sometimes, I'd eventually settle in.

But I didn't. Not right away.
I struggled—**academically, socially, athletically, even leadership-wise.** Not because I wasn't trying, but because I felt like I was doing it all solo. And let's be honest: trying to survive high school without *at least one person who "gets you"* is like trying to win a team sport with no teammates. Exhausting. And kind of sad to watch.

But then, slowly, something shifted.
I found *my people.* Not all at once. Not with confetti or matching friendship bracelets. Just slowly—through group projects, locker conversations, shared jokes that made the school day suck a little less.
And once I had a small circle I trusted?
Everything got better. Still messy. Still awkward. But better.

Not because I became some social butterfly. But because I stopped carrying everything by myself.

REAL TALK: FRIENDSHIPS DON'T NEED A GRAND ENTRANCE

Look—there's no form you fill out that says, *"Yes, I would like to officially have real friends now."* It's usually just a moment—someone who laughs at your joke when no one else does. A partner in biology who actually helps. A random "Hey, wanna sit here?" in the cafeteria that turns into something more.

The right people don't make high school perfect.
But they *do* make it possible.
They help you stay grounded, honest, and encouraged— even on the weird days when your hoodie's too warm and you bomb a quiz and someone *still* calls you by the wrong name.

You don't need to do this alone.
In fact, you're not supposed to.

YOUR TURN TO REFLECT

Take a moment to write honestly. There's no "right" answer here—just real ones.

1. Who is someone I feel safe being myself around?
   (Who doesn't expect me to pretend or perform?)

   _____

   _____

   _____

   _____

   _____

2. What kind of support do I need right now?
   (Are there ways I could reach out or let someone show up for me?)

   _____

   _____

   _____

   _____

   _____

BE THE FRIEND
YOU'RE LOOKING FOR

💬 **TRUTH TO CARRY**

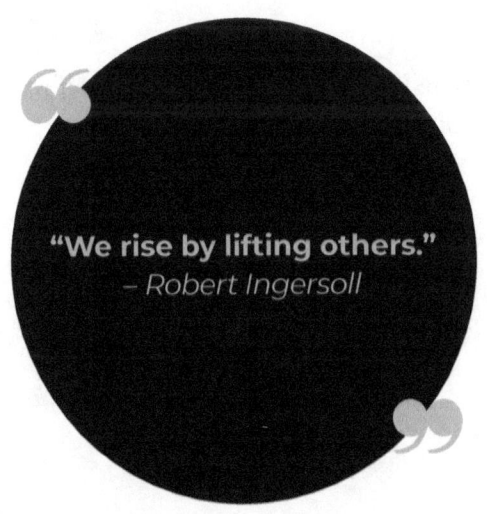

"We rise by lifting others."
– Robert Ingersoll

MY FRESH START: THE BREAKFAST CLUB BLUEPRINT

Let's talk about one of the greatest gifts the '80s gave us: *The Breakfast Club*.

Five high schoolers walk into Saturday detention—a brain, an athlete, a basket case, a princess, and a criminal. Sounds like the setup for a bad joke, right?

But here's the thing—they start off strangers, judging each other by their cliques, but end the day as something closer to... friends. Not because someone gave an inspiring locker room speech. Not because they did a trust fall.

But because they stopped pretending and started *paying attention*.

There's a quote near the end that hits hard—Andrew, the jock, says:
"We're all pretty bizarre. Some of us are just better at hiding it, that's all."

Translation: *Everyone's a little weird. But if you can get past the act, you'll find something real.*

That's the friendship secret right there.

REAL TALK: KINDNESS + CURIOSITY = CONNECTION

You want to find good friends? Here's the hack: **be one.**
The real kind. Not the "let me act like I've got it all together" kind. Not the "I'll only talk to you if your social stock is high" kind. The kind that listens. The kind that says hi first. The kind that stays awkward and shows up anyway.

You don't need to be perfect. You just need to care.

Because you're not the only one feeling left out.
You're not the only one eating lunch hoping someone will say, *"Wanna sit here?"*
And you're definitely not the only one walking the halls wondering if anyone *really* sees you.

Friendship doesn't show up with a neon sign and a trumpet.
It sneaks in through moments of kindness and curiosity.
It starts when you take a breath and say, *"Hey, what's up?"*
It grows when you ask, *"You okay?"* or share your chips at lunch, or just stick around when someone looks like they need company.

Be the friend you're looking for.
You never know who's looking back, hoping for the same thing.

YOUR TURN TO REFLECT

Take a moment to write honestly. There's no "right" answer here—just real ones.

1. What does being a good friend mean to me?
   (What do I hope people feel when they're around me?)

   _____

   _____

   _____

   _____

   _____

2. What's one small thing I could do today to brighten someone's day?
   (A compliment, a message, a moment of kindness—what could I offer?)

   _____

   _____

   _____

   _____

   _____

BOUNDARIES BUILD RESPECT

💬 **TRUTH TO CARRY**

"Daring to set boundaries is about having the courage to love ourselves, even when we risk disappointing others."
— *Brené Brown*

MY FRESH START: 80S HAIR, 80S HEADSPACE

So, yes—I really *did* go to high school in the '80s. And no, we didn't ride dinosaurs to school, but the hair was big, the Walkmans were sacred, and every song seemed to come with some kind of life advice buried in the chorus.

One of those songs?
♫ *"Hold on loosely, but don't let go..."* ♫
Yeah, that was 38 *Special*, 1981. Classic. And honestly? Kinda genius when it comes to freshman friendships, dating, drama—*all of it*.

Because here's what I've seen as a teacher, a coach, and now as someone who speaks to students like you:
Freshmen sometimes cling too tightly.
To friends. To approval. To a crush. To fitting in.
It's like holding a balloon in a windstorm—tight grip, sweaty palms, total panic if it floats away.

Ryan, a student I taught years ago, did this a lot. Great kid, but he didn't know how to say no. He let people copy his work, pressure him into hanging out when he needed rest, even loaned out his new hoodie (big mistake). All because he didn't want to disappoint anyone.

The problem? He *forgot himself* in the process. He was afraid to lose people... and almost lost his peace instead.

REAL TALK: HOLD ON LOOSELY

Boundaries sound like buzzkill rules—but they're actually power moves.

They don't push people away. They protect what matters.

When you say:

⬤ "I need space."

⬤ "That joke isn't funny to me."

⬤ "I'm not okay with that."

You're not being rude—you're being **real**.

And here's the twist: the people who *respect* those boundaries?
They're the ones worth keeping around.
Anyone who ditches you for speaking up... probably wasn't in it for the right reasons anyway.

That song got it right: *"Hold on loosely, but don't let go."*
Let people in—but not so close they erase you.
Love others—but love yourself enough to say, *"Here's what I need."*

Boundaries aren't walls. They're bridges—built on trust, not control.

YOUR TURN TO REFLECT

Take a moment to write honestly. There's no "right" answer here—just real ones.

1. What's one boundary I want to set this year?
    (Where in my life do I need to say "enough" or "not now"?)

    _____

    _____

    _____

    _____

    _____

2. How can I communicate my needs with kindness?
    (What would it sound like to be honest and respectful at the same time?)

    _____

    _____

    _____

    _____

    _____

STAND STRONG AGAINST PRESSURE

💬 **TRUTH TO CARRY**

"Don't compromise yourself. You're all you've got."
– Janis Joplin

MY FRESH START: THE OLDEST STORY ON THE SCREEN

If you've ever watched a classic family sitcom—literally *any* of them—you've seen the peer pressure episode. It's a rite of passage.

One of the kids gets invited to a party they probably shouldn't go to. Or someone dares them to do something ridiculous, like cheat on a test, steal a candy bar, or spray paint Principal Belding's car (*looking at you, Zack Morris*).

The kid caves. Drama unfolds. Moral of the story: *Be yourself. Don't follow the crowd. Cue emotional music. Freeze-frame hug.* Episode over.

Now, you'd think after 70 years of that same plotline, people would have learned something. But nope. Peer pressure is still a thing. And for **freshmen**, it hits harder than a laugh track after a cheesy one-liner.

Why? Because this is the year when most students are still figuring out **who they are.**

When you're not sure of your voice yet, it's easy to borrow someone else's.

And when fitting in feels like the only goal, you'll do just about anything not to stand out.

REAL TALK: DON'T SHRINK TO FIT

Here's the problem: the crowd *never* pays off like you think it will.

You laugh at the joke that makes you uncomfortable, but feel worse later.
You go along with something you know isn't right, and now you're on the hook for a choice you didn't want to make.
You change your style, your words, your vibe—just to blend in—and lose a little piece of yourself every time.

It's not worth it.
Fitting in isn't worth shrinking down.

The people who pressure you to act different? They don't know the real you.
And if they *did* know the real you—and didn't respect it?
That's not your people.

You don't have to yell, fight, or post dramatic quotes on your story.
Just stand. Quietly. Steadily.
A simple, *"Nah, I'm good,"* can be the most powerful sentence you speak this year.

And here's the thing: when you stand strong, others notice.

Someone else who feels pressured might follow your lead.

And *that* is leadership—not a title, but the courage to be yourself.

YOUR TURN TO REFLECT

Take a moment to write honestly. There's no "right" answer here—just real ones.

1. When have I felt pressure to act differently than my values?
   (Was it a moment that didn't sit right, even if no one noticed?)

   _____

   _____

   _____

   _____

   _____

2. What's something I'll stand firm in no matter what?
   (What belief, boundary, or part of who I am won't change based on the crowd?)

   _____

   _____

   _____

   _____

   _____

✳ DAY 20

CHOOSE YOUR CIRCLE

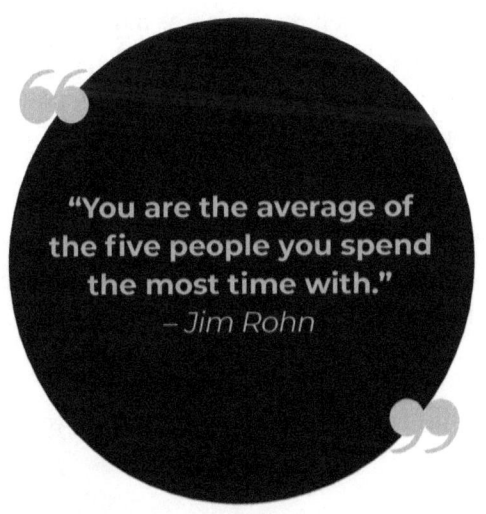

💬 **TRUTH TO CARRY**

"You are the average of the five people you spend the most time with."
– Jim Rohn

MY FRESH START: I COULD SEE IT COMING

This is one of my favorite quotes—ever. Because it's not just clever...
It's **true.**
Scary true.

As a teacher and coach, I could often predict how a student's story would go just by watching who they ran with. I'm talking week one. Day one. **Lunch table. Hallway vibe. Group chat energy.**

If their friends were motivated, kind, and worked hard—*guess what?* They usually rose to that level.
But if their circle was built on cutting class, tearing others down, or celebrating being average?
That student almost always drifted right into that same current.

And they didn't even realize it was happening.
Because here's the thing—**your circle shapes you.**
You think you're just hanging out... but they're shaping your mood, your mindset, and your momentum.

I've seen brilliant students *burn out* because they surrounded themselves with people who didn't care.
And I've seen struggling students *level up* because their circle challenged them to be better.

Your friends are either **fuel** or **friction.**
They're lifting you up—or they're holding you back.

REAL TALK: WHO'S IN YOUR FRONT ROW?

Freshman year is when most people start building their high school crew. It might start with whoever you sit near in class, or who you knew in middle school, or who compliments your hoodie.

That's fine... for a while.

But eventually, you've got to look around and ask:
Are these people helping me grow—or keeping me stuck?

Your closest friends should be:

✔ People who encourage your dreams, not laugh at them.

✔ People who tell the truth—even when it's hard.

✔ People who push you to be better, not pull you into drama. '

✔ People who celebrate your wins, not compete with them.

Choosing your circle doesn't mean ditching everyone who isn't perfect.
It means being **intentional** about who has the most influence in your life.
Because whether you like it or not, their habits, attitudes, and energy *will* rub off on you.

So ask yourself: *Is this who I want to become more like?*
If the answer's no—it might be time to make some moves.

YOUR TURN TO REFLECT

Take a moment to write honestly. There's no "right" answer here—just real ones.

1. Who inspires me to grow?
   (Whose energy pushes me forward in the right direction?)

   _____

   _____

   _____

   _____

   _____

2. What qualities do I want most in my closest friends?
   (If I could build a dream crew—what would they be like?)

   _____

   _____

   _____

   _____

   _____

GIVE WHAT YOU WANT TO RECEIVE

💬 **TRUTH TO CARRY**

"If you want to
lift yourself up, lift up
someone else."
– *Booker T. Washington*

"A generous person will
prosper; whoever refreshes
others will be refreshed."
– *Proverbs 11:25 (NIV)*

MY FRESH START: THE FRIENDSHIP HACK I WISH I KNEW

When I was a freshman, I wanted what every student wants:
Friends who respected me.
People who encouraged me.
A crew who actually cared if I was having a rough day.

But I didn't know how to *find* that. So I waited. I kept hoping someone would notice, invite, include, affirm. Spoiler alert: that strategy? It's like waiting for Chick-fil-A on a Sunday. Not happening.

What I eventually learned—and what Booker T. Washington said so perfectly—is that if you want to lift *yourself* up... **start by lifting someone else.**

That truth has been around a long time.
Proverbs 11:25 puts it this way:
"Whoever refreshes others will be refreshed."

In other words:

➡️ Want more kindness? Be kind first.

➡️ Want people to notice you? Start noticing *them*.

➡️ Want encouragement? Speak it into others.

Because what you put out into the world? It usually circles back.

REAL TALK: BECOME WHAT YOU'RE LOOKING FOR

Too often, we sit around thinking:
"No one's there for me."
"No one checks in."
"No one really sees me."

But what if someone else is thinking the *exact same thing,* waiting for you to make the first move?

Freshman year is full of people who are lonely, uncertain, and hoping someone will show up for them. That someone might be **you**.

Instead of asking, *"Why doesn't anyone support me?"*
Flip it. Ask: *"Who can I support today?"*

Respect, kindness, encouragement—these aren't things you have to wait to receive. They're things you can choose to *give,* right now.

And here's the magic:
You don't just lift others when you do this...
You lift yourself.

Your confidence grows.
Your self-image deepens.
Your circle gets stronger.
All because you chose to *go first.*

YOUR TURN TO REFLECT

Take a moment to write honestly. There's no "right" answer here—just real ones.

1. What do I want more of in my friendships?
   (Respect? Laughter? Loyalty? Encouragement? Be honest.)

   _____

   _____

   _____

   _____

   _____

2. How can I give that to someone else today?
   (What small act, text, smile, or encouragement can I share first?

   _____

   _____

   _____

   _____

   _____

RELATIONSHIPS REFLECTION: YOUR PEOPLE, YOUR PATH

💬 TRUTH TO CARRY

"The most beautiful discovery true friends make is that they can grow separately without growing apart."
– Elisabeth Foley

THE REAL MVPS OF HIGH SCHOOL

Let's go! You've just wrapped an entire week focused on one of the most powerful forces in your high school journey: **relationships**. Not just finding them—but choosing, building, and investing in the *right* ones.

You've reflected on boundaries, peer pressure, kindness, influence, and what it means to *actually be* the friend you're hoping to find. That's big. That's deep. And if you did the work this week—*even just a little bit*—you're already better because of it.

Here's the thing no one tells you in the welcome packet:
Your people shape your path.
They can build you up, break you down, or keep you stuck. And choosing the right ones isn't just a "nice idea"—it's a game-changer.

But here's something even more real:
Even the best relationships get messy.
Even your closest friends will grow in different directions.
But strong friendships? They don't fall apart just because things change.
They flex. They stretch. They grow *with* you—not just *next* to you.

REAL TALK: GROW TOGETHER, NOT APART

Freshman year is full of shifting circles—some friends fade, some show up unexpectedly, and others grow into something deeper than you imagined. That's normal.

The goal isn't to find people who are exactly like you, or to lock into a friendship contract with no room for growth. The goal is to surround yourself with people who challenge you to be better—and love you even when you're figuring it out.

People who clap when you win.
Check on you when you're quiet.
Call you out when you're off.
And let you do the same for them.

Those friendships don't just happen.
They're built—over time, with real talk, honest moments, and showing up when it's not easy.

So here's your challenge:
Keep doing the work.
Don't settle for surface-level friends when deeper ones are waiting to be built.
Don't ghost people who matter just because things get uncomfortable.
And don't be afraid to outgrow what's not growing with you.

Your people will shape your path. Choose them wisely. Love them well.

YOUR TURN TO REFLECT

Take a moment to write honestly. There's no "right" answer here—just real ones.

1. What friendship or connection grew this week?
    (Did you notice someone show up for you? Did you show up for someone else?)

    _____

    _____

    _____

    _____

2. What kind of relationship do you want to continue building this year?
    (What do you want more of—honesty, fun, trust, depth? Who might you build that with?)

    _____

    _____

    _____

    _____

    _____

🎯 WEEK 4

GOAL SETTING — *"SHAPE YOUR FUTURE"*

Weekly Quote: *"You were never created to live depressed, defeated, guilty, condemned, ashamed or unworthy. You were created to be victorious."*

– Unknown

DREAM BIG, START SMALL

💬 **TRUTH TO CARRY**

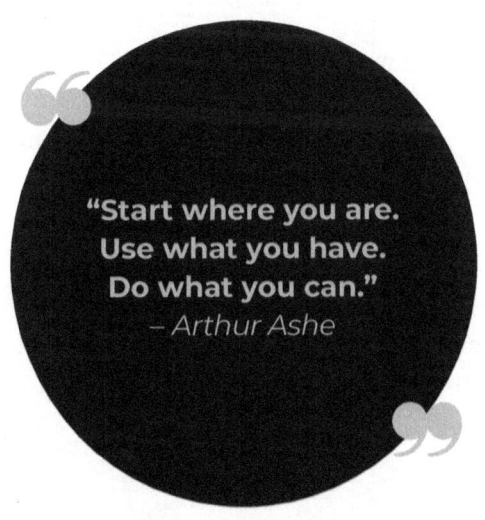

"Start where you are.
Use what you have.
Do what you can."
– Arthur Ashe

FROM THE DESK OF SOMEONE WHO'S ASKED THOUSANDS OF FRESHMEN

Here's something I've done for **over three decades:**
I've looked freshmen in the eye—quiet ones, loud ones, honors students, athletes, gamers, artists, all of them—and asked this question:
"What's your dream?"

And you'd be shocked how many of them stop like a deer in headlights.
Not because they don't *have* a dream...
But because it's the **first time anyone's actually asked.**

Most students walk into high school carrying goals—but they're not always their *own* goals.
Parents want honor roll.
Coaches want championships.
Teachers want effort.
And peers? They want you to fit in and keep up.

But what do *you* want?
What lights you up inside?
What future would you chase if no one was watching your report card or your stat line?

That's the question.
THE question.

Because high school isn't just about completing tasks.
It's about discovering—and *building*—the kind of life you want to live.

REAL TALK: BIG DREAMS ARE BUILT IN SMALL MOMENTS

Here's what I've learned after hearing hundreds of freshman answers:
Dreams don't always come out loud and confident.
Sometimes they whisper.
Sometimes they sound crazy, impossible, or way out of reach.
But every dream worth chasing has one thing in common: a **starting point.**

You don't need to map the whole journey.
You just need to take one step.

Whether it's trying out for a team, starting a YouTube channel, speaking up in class, writing a song, getting a part-time job, or working toward a 4.0—it all starts with one choice to move.

You don't have to be perfect.
You don't have to be ready.
You just have to be willing to begin.

So today, pause the noise, tune out the pressure, and answer the question for *you.*
What do *you* want?

YOUR TURN TO REFLECT

Take a moment to write honestly. There's no "right" answer here—just real ones.

1. What's one big dream I have for my high school years? (Forget what others expect—what would I love to do or become?)

_____

_____

_____

_____

_____

2. What small step could I take toward that this week? (What simple action would move me just a little closer?)

_____

_____

_____

_____

_____

DEFINE THE "WHY"

"Working hard for something we don't care about is called stress; working hard for something we love is called passion."
— *Simon Sinek*

THE WHY BEHIND THE WORK

Simon Sinek is a leadership expert, bestselling author, and the guy behind the wildly popular idea: **"Start with why."**
And this quote? It hits *hard* in high school—especially for freshmen.

Think about it:
You've got homework. Practice. Group projects. Tests.
Schedules stacked higher than your backpack.
And half the time, you're wondering: *"Why am I even doing this?"*

Here's what Sinek teaches:
When we **work hard** for something that doesn't matter to us, it feels like pressure.
But when we **work hard** for something we believe in?
It becomes *purpose.*
It's not just about checking boxes. It's about **chasing something real.**

REAL TALK: STRESS OR PASSION— WHAT'S FUELING YOU?

Freshman year is when the pressure can sneak in from every direction—parents, teachers, coaches, even your own expectations. Everyone's asking:

- ☑ "What's your GPA?"
- ☑ "Are you trying out?"

☑ "Did you turn it in?"

But almost no one is asking:
"Why are you doing this in the first place?"

Your *why* is your anchor.
It's the reason behind your goals.
And without it? Even something small can feel overwhelming.
But when your *why* is clear—when it *matters* to you personally—it changes the game.

Studying for a test becomes a step toward your dream job.
Practicing a speech becomes part of your purpose to lead.
Trying out for the team becomes more than making the roster—it becomes proving something to yourself.

Sinek says this too:

"People don't buy what you do, they buy *why* you do it."
The same is true for *you*.
You don't stay motivated just because of the goal.
You stay motivated because of the *reason* behind it.

So let's stop doing things just because someone said we "should."
Let's find the fire underneath.
Let's define your *why*—and let it drive you.

YOUR TURN TO REFLECT

Take a moment to write honestly. There's no "right" answer here—just real ones.

1. Why does this goal matter deeply to me—not just in my head, but in my heart?
   (What belief, dream, or emotion is connected to it?)

   _____

   _____

   _____

   _____

   _____

2. How might reaching this goal impact my future or the people around me?
   (How could this ripple outward—into my life, my family, my friends?)

   _____

   _____

   _____

   _____

   _____

ZIGLAR GOALS, PART 1: DEFINE & BENEFITS

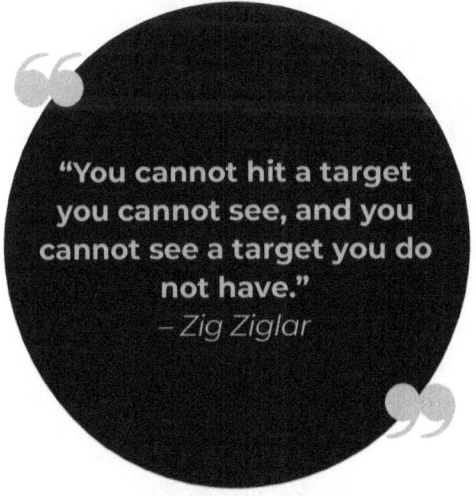

"You cannot hit a target you cannot see, and you cannot see a target you do not have."
– Zig Ziglar

THE LEGEND LAYS IT OUT

Zig Ziglar is a legend in the world of personal growth and motivation. He was the kind of speaker who could get a room full of adults on their feet—and he made *goal setting* sound like a superpower instead of a boring classroom assignment.

His message? Simple but powerful:
If you want to hit a goal, you've got to name it—and know why it matters.

Freshmen often make vague goals like:
"I want to do better."
"I want to be successful."
"I want to make my parents proud."

Okay, cool. But Zig would ask: *What does that actually mean?*
How will you know if you're on track? If you've "made it"?

That's where his goal-setting method starts—with two critical first steps:

STEP ONE: IDENTIFY YOUR GOAL CLEARLY

Not kinda-sorta. Not *"I guess I want to..."*
We're talking crystal clear.
Not "get good grades," but *"earn a B or higher in every class."*
Not "be healthier," but *"exercise three times a week."*
Not "be more social," but *"invite one person to sit with me this week."*

Zig said, "You cannot hit a target you cannot see."
So stop aiming blind. Start aiming *real*.

 ## STEP TWO: LIST THE BENEFITS

Here's where it gets exciting.
When you know *why* the goal matters—what's at stake, what's waiting on the other side—it changes how you chase it.

Ask yourself:

- ☑ What will improve if I hit this goal?

- ☑ How will I feel?

- ☑ What doors will open?

- ☑ Who will be proud (including me)?

Zig believed that motivation isn't just about effort. It's about clarity. When the **benefits** are clear, the drive becomes real.

This is your moment to pause, focus, and say:
This is what I want.
And this is why it matters.

YOUR TURN TO REFLECT

Take a moment to write honestly. There's no "right" answer here—just real ones.

1. What exactly do I want to achieve this semester? (Be specific—grades, habits, goals, growth. What's the target?)

_____

_____

_____

_____

_____

2. What will improve in my life if I achieve it? (Think about the benefits—how will this goal make your life better?)

_____

_____

_____

_____

_____

ZIGLAR GOALS, PART 2: OBSTACLES & KNOWLEDGE

💬 **TRUTH TO CARRY**

"Success is when preparation meets opportunity."
– Seneca

TRIPPING BEFORE YOU TRIUMPH

Let's be real: if your goals were going to chase *themselves*, they'd be done by now.

Zig Ziglar knew that hitting your goals isn't just about dreaming big—it's about **preparing for the roadblocks**. Because every dream has at least one "oops," "ugh," or "are you kidding me?"

Welcome to **Ziglar Steps 3 & 4**:

→ Identify the obstacles

→ List the knowledge and skills you'll need to overcome them

Let's break it down.

STEP THREE: IDENTIFY THE OBSTACLES

Picture this:
You've got your goal locked in. You're pumped. You're focused. You're ready to conquer the world.

Then BOOM.

Here comes the first *obstacle*.

Maybe it's...

A math class that feels like it's written in an alien language

A friend who texts *"Wanna hang?"* every time you try to study

🌀 A bad habit of saying *"I'll start tomorrow"*

🌀 Or that tiny voice whispering *"You're not good enough"*

If you **don't** call those obstacles out? They'll trip you when you least expect it.
But if you **do**? You can prep for them like a boss.

Zig didn't say obstacles were bad—he just said **don't let them sneak up on you.**

STEP FOUR: GET WHAT YOU NEED

Once you know what might block you, it's time to build your toolbox.

This is where you ask:
"What do I need to learn, practice, or get better at to crush this goal?"

Do you need:

📖 A tutor?

🖩 A study app?

🧠 Better time management?

🤝 Someone to hold you accountable when motivation dips?

Even superheroes need training montages, okay?
Batman has gadgets. Spider-Man had mentors. You need **skills, support, and strategy.**

Preparation turns *"maybe someday"* into *"I'm ready right now."*

The more you know, the more confident you feel when the opportunity shows up.

YOUR TURN TO REFLECT

Take a moment to write honestly. There's no "right" answer here—just real ones.

1. What might stand in the way of my goal?
   (What habits, challenges, or situations could slow me down?)

   _____

   _____

   _____

   _____

   _____

2. What new skills or help will I need to reach it?
   (What can I learn, practice, or ask for that would move me forward?)

   _____

   _____

   _____

   _____

   _____

ZIGLAR GOALS, PART 3: WHO & HOW

"Alone we can do so little; together we can do so much."
– Helen Keller

ZIGLAR GOALS: THE FINAL ROUND

Alright—if you've made it this far, you are officially past the "dream about it" phase and deep into the *"let's make this thing happen"* zone.

You've:

☑ Named the goal

☑ Listed the benefits

☑ Called out the obstacles

☑ Identified what skills or knowledge you'll need

Now it's time to finish what Zig started—with his **final three steps:**

⑤ *Who can support you*

⑥ *Create an action plan*

⑦ *Set a timeline*

Let's roll.

 # STEP FIVE: FIND YOUR HYPE SQUAD

Here's a fact: doing big things solo is overrated.

Even superheroes have sidekicks. Even the best athletes have coaches. And even your favorite YouTubers have a behind-the-scenes team editing their bloopers.

So ask yourself:
Who can keep me focused when I want to quit?
Who believes in me enough to call me out?
Who will remind me WHY I started in the first place?

That's your **goal squad**. Text them. Talk to them. Let them in on the plan.

🎯 STEP SIX: BUILD THE PLAN

A goal without a plan is just a wish.
So... how are you going to make this happen?

Break it down:

☞ What's the first step?

☞ Then what?

☞ And what's something you can actually do **this week**?

You don't need a 42-point spreadsheet—just a basic plan that says:
"I'm going to do this. Then that. Then keep going."

Even if it's messy—**movement beats perfection.**

⏰ STEP SEVEN: SET A TIMELINE

Goals love **deadlines**. Why?
Because "someday" is code for "never."

When you say:
"I'll start eventually," what you *really* mean is:

"I'll forget by Friday."

So give your dream a date.
This month. This semester. This week.
Say it. Write it. Stick it on your mirror.
Time plus action = momentum.

ZIG WOULD BE PROUD

Zig Ziglar believed in ordinary people doing extraordinary things.
Not because they were perfect.
But because they were clear. Committed. And willing to move.

That's you now.

So go build the dream—one person, one plan, one timeline at a time.

YOUR TURN TO REFLECT

Take a moment to write honestly. There's no "right" answer here—just real ones.

1. Who can help me stay motivated?
   (Who's in my corner—family, friend, teacher, coach?)

   _____

   _____

   _____

   _____

   _____

2. What's one action I can take this week to move forward?
   (Even one small move can create momentum. What's mine?)

   _____

   _____

   _____

   _____

   _____

KEEP IT MOVING

💬 **TRUTH TO CARRY**

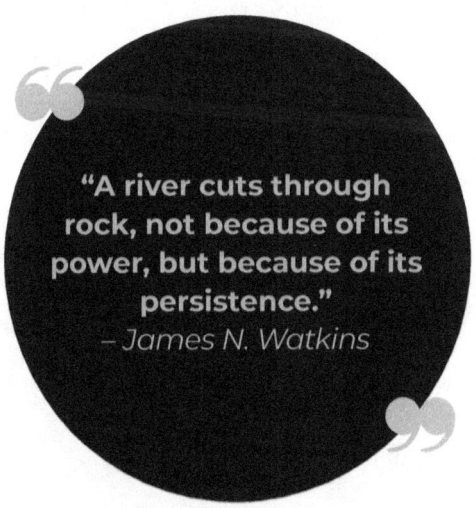

"A river cuts through rock, not because of its power, but because of its persistence."
– *James N. Watkins*

WATCHING THE WORK GET DONE

A while back, I gave my son a job to do in our yard. Not one of those "just sweep this real quick" jobs.
Nope—this was **tedious, slow, shoulder-sore, full-sun, why-do-we-even-have-a-yard** kind of work.

I told him what needed to be done, handed him the tools, and honestly thought: *"Well, this could go sideways real fast."*

But what I saw amazed me.

He didn't try to rush it.
He didn't overthink it.
He just... started.
Little by little, chunk by chunk.
Clearing. Hauling. Taking breaks. Getting back at it.
No dramatic music. No applause. Just consistent, steady, show-up-and-work kind of effort.

And when he finished?
We both stood there like—*Whoa.*
He'd made a massive job look *shockingly* simple.
Not because it *was* easy...
But because he kept moving, even when it wasn't.

REAL TALK: PERSISTENCE WINS

That's what this day is all about.

High school goals, friendships, tough classes, big dreams—they won't all move fast.
They won't all feel epic.

But progress doesn't need to scream. It just needs to keep going.

You don't need to be the loudest.
Or the fastest.
Or the best.
You just need to **be the one who doesn't stop.**

Because the people who finish strong?
They're not always the ones with the head start.
They're the ones who stayed in the race.
Who took breaks but came back.
Who had rough days but didn't let those days *end the story*.

That quote says it best:
"A river cuts through rock, not because of its power, but because of its persistence."

Translation:
Be the river.
Not flashy. Not perfect. Just *relentless*.

YOUR TURN TO REFLECT

Take a moment to write honestly. There's no "right" answer here—just real ones.

1. What has helped me keep going even when it's hard?
    (A person? A mindset? A habit? What's kept me steady?)

_____

_____

_____

_____

_____

2. What's my next step, no matter how small?
    (Even tiny moves move you forward—what's mine today?)

_____

_____

_____

_____

_____

GOAL SETTING REFLECTION: FROM VISION TO ACTION

💬 **TRUTH TO CARRY**

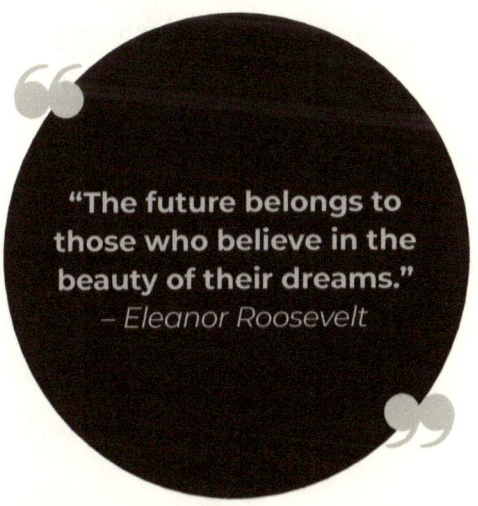

"The future belongs to those who believe in the beauty of their dreams."
– Eleanor Roosevelt

FROM "SOMEDAY" TO "LET'S GO"

Let's take a second to clap it up—you've made it through a week of honest, sometimes awkward, occasionally energizing, and always important goal-setting work. And if you're still here, still writing, still dreaming? That says something.

You're not just talking about it.
You're doing something most people skip:
You're turning *dreams* into *decisions*.
And *decisions* into *action*.

This week wasn't about becoming perfect.
It was about becoming clear.

You've:

☑ Named what matters to you

☑ Faced what might stand in your way

☑ Gathered the knowledge and support you'll need

☑ Built a plan

☑ Taken real steps

And now... you're standing at the edge of possibility with *momentum on your side.*

REAL TALK: DREAMS AREN'T MAGIC— THEY'RE MUSCLE

Here's something you need to know: **dreams are great—but they aren't magic.**

They don't transform into reality just because you think hard enough or write them in your notes app surrounded by ✥sparkles✥.

They come to life when you *move*.
Every big achievement?
It started with someone making a decision:
"I'm going to show up again."
"I'm going to learn from that fail."
"I'm going to do what I said I'd do—even if I don't feel like it."

And yeah, your goals might change. That's okay.
What matters is that you don't sit on the sidelines waiting for someone else to hand you your dream.
You start building it. With what you have. From where you are.

Even if it's clunky. Even if you're scared. Even if you don't have all the steps yet.
Because here's the deal:
You don't have to be *ready*.
You just have to be *willing*.

A QUICK ZIGLAR THROWBACK

Zig Ziglar said it best:

"What you get by achieving your goals is not as important as what you become by achieving your goals."

That's the *real* win—you becoming stronger, wiser, more focused, and more *you*.

YOUR TURN TO REFLECT

Take a moment to write honestly. There's no "right" answer here—just real ones.

1. What goal feels more real to me now than it did a week ago?
   (Have I taken a step that made it feel possible—or even probable?)

   _____

   _____

   _____

   _____

   _____

2. What will I commit to continuing next month?
   (What goal, habit, or mindset do I want to keep building on?)

   _____

   _____

   _____

   _____

   _____

 **DAY 30**

FINAL DAY: YOU'RE JUST GETTING STARTED

💬 **TRUTH TO CARRY**

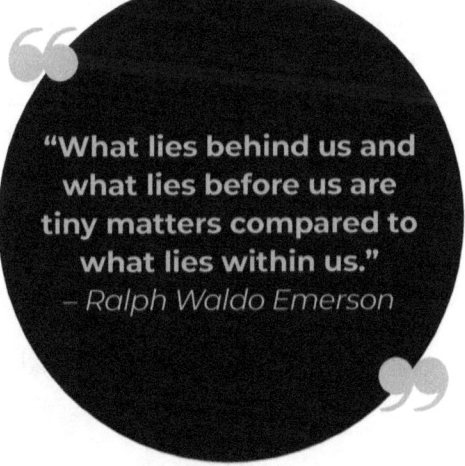

"What lies behind us and what lies before us are tiny matters compared to what lies within us."
— *Ralph Waldo Emerson*

THE FINAL PAGE (BUT NOT THE END)

You made it.

30 days.
30 pages of thoughts, stories, goals, and let's be honest—some serious soul-searching.
And if you're thinking, *"Wow, that was a lot..."*
You're absolutely right.

Because this wasn't just a journal. It was a launchpad.
And this last page?
It's not the finish line—it's the **starting block**.

Let's rewind for a second:
You began this journey trying to open your locker without crying.
You weren't sure what crowd you'd fit in with, what dreams were actually *yours*, or what it even meant to "be yourself" without totally overthinking it.

You learned that being scared is normal.
That confidence doesn't come before the leap—it *grows* from the leap.
That comparison is a trap, but your story still matters.
That your inner voice can either coach you or crush you—and it's worth rewiring.
You saw how your people shape your path.
That boundaries aren't rude—they're smart.
That kindness builds connection.
That big dreams need small steps.
And that goals? They don't work unless *you* do.

Remember Clark? The quiet kid who didn't think his voice mattered—until it did.

Or your son, clearing that massive yard, little by little, until the job was done.

Or Ryan, who tried to fake it till he flopped—but kept going anyway.

And yes, remember *me*—the 5'4", 115-pound freshman who missed shots, failed auditions, got cut from teams, and struck out asking girls to dances.

But also the guy who kept showing up.

Not because I had it all together, but because I believed someday I *might*.

REAL TALK: THE BECOMING CONTINUES

This month wasn't about being perfect.

It was about becoming **clearer**, **stronger**, and more **rooted** in who you are and where you're going.

You're not finished—you're **prepared**.
And no matter how shaky this month felt...
you've built something real.
Now it's time to carry it forward.

You *will* have rough days.
But now you've got tools.
You *will* have doubts.
But now you've got truth.
You *will* face pressure.
But now you've got purpose.

Keep becoming.
Keep stepping.
Keep dreaming.
Because you, my friend, are just getting started.

YOUR TURN TO REFLECT

Take a moment to write honestly. There's no "right" answer here—just real ones.

1. What have I discovered about myself this month?
    (What surprised me? What grew stronger?)

    _____

    _____

    _____

    _____

    _____

2. What do I want to carry with me for the rest of freshman year?
    (What truth, belief, or goal will I hold on to when things get tough?)

    _____

    _____

    _____

    _____

    _____

● FINAL THOUGHTS FROM ME TO YOU

If you've made it to the end of this journal—WOW. I'm impressed. Not just because you stuck with it, but because you *showed up for yourself,* day after day.

This was never about filling space. It was about building something—inside you.

And let me tell you what I see now:
I see someone stronger.
Someone more self-aware.
Someone who can think bigger, love deeper, and walk through these high school halls with more purpose than they started with.

You may not see that yet—but I do.
I've worked with students for a long time, and I've seen what can happen when someone like you decides to lean in, reflect, and grow.

You're not just "getting through" freshman year.
You're *becoming.*

✴ ZIG SAID IT BEST...

One of my favorite quotes comes from the one and only **Zig Ziglar**:

> *"You were born to win, but to be a winner, you must plan to win, prepare to win, and expect to win."*

That's not just motivational poster stuff. That's truth—especially for you.

Because here's what most people miss:
Being "born to win" doesn't mean it's automatic.
It means the potential is already *in you*—but it only shows up when you decide to work with it.

And guess what?
This journal?
It was your **plan**.
Your **preparation**.
Your first big step toward expecting more from yourself this year—and believing it's actually possible.

So if you've ever felt like you're behind, not enough, or unsure what your purpose is...
I just want to say with 100% certainty:
You have what it takes.
Right now. Not someday.
Today. This year.

I'M PRAYING FOR YOU. I BELIEVE IN YOU.

I may not know your name, your schedule, or how weird your gym locker smells, but I promise you this:
I'm praying for you.
Not just for good grades or perfect friend groups—though those are nice—but for *real growth*.
For moments when you discover something powerful about yourself.
For confidence that builds quietly over time.
And for boldness to step up when it matters most.

I believe in you.
I'm excited for you.
And I'm confident you can become all you were made to be.
Even if you can't see it yet—I *can*.

THIS ISN'T GOODBYE

Just because you've finished the journal doesn't mean the journey ends here.

This was your warm-up.
Now the real stuff begins: walking into school with intention, kindness, purpose, and grit.
You've got the tools now. And I can't wait to see how you use them.

Also...
Don't be a stranger.

Seriously—reach out.

Say hi. Tell me what stuck with you. Share your wins, your struggles, your progress, your proud moments, your "I DID IT" breakthroughs.

I'd love to hear how things are going.

Because I'm not just cheering for you from a distance—I'm *in this with you.*

You've got this.

Freshman year is just your first chapter.

Now go make it unforgettable.

– James 🙌

ABOUT THE AUTHOR

James McLamb is a passionate communicator, youth advocate, and founder of Generation Youth. With a unique blend of classroom experience and entrepreneurial leadership, James has dedicated his life to equipping and inspiring the next generation. His work is deeply  influenced by the legacy of Zig Ziglar, blending timeless values with real-world strategies to help young people thrive.

James is the creator of the Generation Youth Coaching Certification, a powerful program designed to equip educators, life coaches, and leaders to effectively mentor and empower youth. His practical, heart-led approach has made him one of the nation's go-to experts in youth development.

A former high school agriculture teacher, James holds degrees from North Carolina State University and Clemson University in Agricultural Education and Youth Development Leadership. He's the author of *Tomorrow's Youth* and host of The Generation Youth Podcast, where he shares stories, insights, and tools to help young people grow in confidence and purpose.

James lives in North Carolina with his wife of 30 years, Melissa, and their three children—Sara Beth, Jacob, and Abby.

To connect with James or invite him to speak at your event, reach out at james@generationziglar.com.

🚀 KEEP GROWING WITH THE IGNITE: 30-DAY SERIES

FRESHMAN → SOPHOMORE → JUNIOR → SENIOR

📖 Loved this book? There's more where that came from. Whether you're just starting your journey or nearing the finish line, we've got a powerful 30-day experience designed just for your stage of high school life.

👓 Sneak Peek + Samples Available!
Visit: www.generation-youth.com/ignite30day
You'll find:

- ▨ Freshman Year Journal: *Mindset, Self-Image, Relationships, Goals*

- ▨ Sophomore Year Journal: *Growth Mindset, Handling Negativity, Peer Pressure & Purpose*

- ▨ Junior Year Journal: *Confidence, Gratitude, Family & Dreaming Big*

- ☐ Senior Year Journal: *Purpose, Resilience, Legacy & Launching Well*

Each 30-day book is packed with:

- ☑ ⬦ Daily Motivational Quotes
- ☑ 📖 Real-Life Stories & Truth
- ☑ ✍ Personal Reflection Prompts
- ☑ 🎯 Weekly Challenges
- ☑ 💬 Journal Spaces for Growth

🎁 WANT TO GO EVEN DEEPER?

Check out our **IGNITE Enhancement Package**
You'll gain access to:

- 📝 Lesson Plans

- 🎨 Extra Journal Prompts

- 🖼 Printable Quote Posters

- 📂 Digital Downloads for Teachers & Parents

Perfect for:
- ➡ Small Groups
- ➡ Youth Coaches
- ➡ Homeschool Co-Ops
- ➡ Classroom Integration

SCAN ME TO EXPLORE

Use your phone camera to scan the QR code below

Instantly access the full Ignite series + enhancement bundle

You've just scratched the surface of who you're becoming. Let's keep the fire going.

www.generation-youth.com/ignite30day

www.ingramcontent.com/pod-product-compliance
Lightning Source LLC
Chambersburg PA
CBHW031531120626
46545CB00005B/2094